Preventing Fraud in Church Accounting

Preventing Fraud in Church Accounting

Common Problems and Practical Solutions
that Church Leaders Can't Afford to Ignore

Lee Ann Crockett

With Foreword by
Bryant Truitt, MBA, CCS, CFE

Preventing Fraud in Church Accounting: Common Problems and Practical Solutions that Church Leaders Can't Afford to Ignore

Copyright © 2018 by Lee Ann Crockett. All Rights Reserved.

Published by Lee Ann Crockett.
Printed in the United States of America

No part of this publication may be reproduced, distributed, or transmitted in any printed or electronic form without the prior written permission of the author, except for brief quotations.

All Scripture quotations, unless otherwise indicated, are taken from the Holy Bible, New International Version®, NIV®. Copyright ©1973, 1978, 1984, 2011 by Biblica, Inc.™ Used by permission of Zondervan. All rights reserved worldwide. www.zondervan.com The "NIV" and "New International Version" are trademarks registered in the United States Patent and Trademark Office by Biblica, Inc.™

Contents

Foreword — vii
Preface — ix

PART I. COMMON PROBLEMS

1. Lack of Time and Resources — 3
2. Lack of Knowledge — 11
3. Lack of Controls: Embezzlement, Fraud, and Theft — 17

PART II. PRACTICAL SOLUTIONS

4. Internal Controls — 27
5. Budget Planning and Review — 35
6. Formal Financial Processes and Reports — 39
7. Considerations Going Forward — 45

About the Author — 51
Bellwether Church Solutions — 53

Foreword

For over 20 years, I have worked as a Certified Fraud Examiner and with each investigation I think, "Well I have seen it all" only to find that there is some new way that an employee, volunteer, or family member has figured out how to defraud or embezzle the church. The statistics are staggering.

And yet, it is almost impossible for church leadership to believe that it could happen to them — until it does. Crisis prevention should be the focus of every non-profit and not crisis management after the fact.

Please take the next few minutes to read this book. It's hard for a Pastor to ask the right questions when he doesn't have the business background and thus the skill set necessary to protect the church from financial fraud. It's just not in their nature to put internal controls in place when "friends" are doing the work.

But take it from me — whether it's the first $50 or $500,000+, theft is happening in over one-third of non-profits this year. Put the policies and procedures in place to minimize the chances of this happening to you. Don't depend solely on the office manager or the administrative assistant to take care of the financial business for your church or you may not have a church to take care of.

FOREWORD

Lee Ann has laid it out for you here – the common problems and some straight-forward solutions that you should consider. Take my advice. Read the book. Be proactive now and avoid the heartache later. And in the meantime, trust but verify.

Bryant Truitt, MBA, CCS, CFE
Brytan & Associates, Inc.
Embezzlement Investigations

Preface

It was mid-morning one spring when I received a phone call from an old acquaintance who was pastoring a church near me. I could tell immediately from the tenor of his voice that something was wrong.

After pleasantries, he began unraveling his story. The church leadership team had just discovered that the treasurer was embezzling from the church. They weren't sure how much or how long, but it appeared to have been going on for several months.

It had come to light as one of the other ministry leaders went to make a purchase with the church credit card and it was declined. How could that be? Their church policy was to pay the balance each month so why would the charge be declined?

The treasurer had been providing spreadsheets each month to the leadership team with income and expenditure information. Everything looked fine. Paychecks were being processed as they should be. The bank account seemed to have funds. It all looked healthy.

But what they didn't know was the treasurer had been using his church debit card for months making personal purchases that ranged

PREFACE

from gasoline and Starbucks to his electricity bill. He had quit paying the church's credit card bill and payroll taxes, and he was not maintaining accurate donation records.

These revelations were heartbreaking — for the pastor, the leadership, the congregation, and me. This was a man who had been known for years by the leadership. He was a founding member of this congregation. Everybody loved him. This act of betrayal was beyond anyone's imagination.

"How does this happen?" I wondered. *"This must be a rare event. Surely this was just a fluke."*

I'm afraid not my dear reader. After the shock subsided, I began investigating to determine how common fraud or embezzlement is perpetrated in our churches. I was sure it must be the exception rather than the rule.

I was stunned.

Thirty percent of all churches experience this breach of trust and in just the first half of 2014, it was reported more than $39 billion was stolen in church-related fraud.[1]

This newfound knowledge mixed with my friend's experience lit a fire in me. Never dreaming I would write a book, I found myself compelled to do so. I couldn't bear it. I wept for this offense against God and His people. My mind was racing as to how we could shore up our defenses against this attack; or better yet, how could we plug this fissure in the church's business. This was the birth of my new focus for Bellwether Church Solutions: educating church leadership about this problem and providing the resources to combat it.

PREFACE

It is my sincere prayer that this little book will be the impetus to ensure that your congregation never experiences this heartbreak of deception and betrayal.

Be on guard! Be alert! You do not know when that time will come. It's like a man going away: He leaves his house and puts his servants in charge, each with their assigned task, and tells the one at the door to keep watch.
Mark 13:33-34

Notes

1. http://www.sharefaith.com/blog/2015/09/18-church-embezzlement/ by Patricia Lotich

PART I

Common Problems

1

Lack of Time and Resources

So the Twelve gathered all the disciples together and said, "It would not be right for us to neglect the ministry of the word of God in order to wait on tables. ..."
Acts 6:2

A pastor graduates from seminary with maybe one semester of business experience. This seems appropriate, doesn't it? Perhaps even generous. A pastor's calling is to spread the Gospel, make disciples of Christ, and minister to the poor — not handle the church financials, board meetings, and building maintenance. In many churches, however, the pastor must wear many hats.

Perusing job descriptions for pastors, I discovered a current posting for a well-known non-denominational church organization. This was a rather lengthy "job" description divided into Pastoral Care, Program Responsibilities, and Administrative Responsibilities. After the standard worship, preaching, and teaching details that I expected to see, I read he is to act in an "advisory" capacity to all staff, members, and boards. He is the operating head of the church delegating all assignments. He is to be the spiritual leader and administrator for all church functions and responsible for "organizing, planning, and controlling the fulfillment of all church programs."

Seriously! This is a "short" summary of the lengthy classified posting – quite an array of responsibilities, isn't it? With this in view, we're reminded that pastoring is not just a job but rather a calling. It is a divine purpose with an eternal reckoning to God for the care and keeping of His flock. The biblical metaphor for a pastor is shepherd. Consider all shepherding entails:

- Ensuring food is available for today
- Finding new pastures
- Watching for predators and poisonous plants
- Keeping a constant head count
- Maintaining the pen
- Caring for the sick and injured
- Protecting the flock in the winter
- Taking care of newborns in the spring

A shepherd spends his life from youth to adulthood living and learning all the skills necessary to care for the flock. But this may be where the metaphor fails.

While a pastor may have been spiritually prepared for his work since youth, it is not likely that he has mastered all of the other responsibilities that the congregation looks to him to oversee. His one-semester seminary course in Church Management covered human resources, administrative practices, and financial matters. Hopefully, he learned enough in that semester to function as the job description referred to earlier required:

- Oversee church financial matters
- Manage all areas of ministry
- Supervise, support, and evaluate staff
- Preside over meetings to coordinate ministries
- Ensure the church facilities are functioning

Who knew pastor was "Greek" for the Financial Controller, the Program Coordinator, the Business Manager, the Facilities Supervisor, and sometimes the Janitor. Each of these positions could be a fulltime job in and of itself and each takes time and energy from his primary purpose as spiritual leader.

Delegation is the only way that he can manage the fulfillment of these responsibilities. If a pastor fails to delegate or has no one to delegate to, his ability to fulfill his calling will be hindered and the administrative duties will also suffer. But does the pastor even feel qualified to delegate the roles he knows the least about? Does he know enough to ask the right questions to ensure his delegates know their job?

Part of this delegating is inherently difficult because churches are often staffed with volunteers. Nine out of 10 churches in America have an average worship attendance of less than 350.[1] This makes for a small candidate pool to find qualified and experienced volunteers to handle some of these essential functions required to maintain a healthy church.

This book is concerned with the pastor's responsibility as the CFO of a church. Because this particular role is labor intensive — involving budgeting, bookkeeping, and reporting — it's natural for the pastor and leadership team to seek out a volunteer they trust. Unfortunately, this is the greatest area of church mismanagement. One report suggests that in just the first six months of one reporting year $59 billion was stolen from churches.[2]

Shocking! Yet, church financial fraud is thriving, and it is estimated that up to 80 percent of these cases go unreported.[3] Why aren't they reported? There is debate as to whether or not it is the "Christianly" thing to do to bring civil law into this situation. Then there is the matter of having your congregation lose faith in the leadership if this happens. And let's not forget the sin of pride; who wants the world to know they were swindled?

Patricia Lotich, the founder of Smart Church Management, reports "church thieves are creative and take advantage of no written policies and haphazard oversight." She goes on to describe that it is difficult for church leaders to wrap their head around a trusted church member stealing from them. She points out that church theft is often by one of the most trusted persons in the church, and most fraud goes undetected for 18 months with the thief having an average tenure of eight years in the church. Researchers expect church financial fraud to reach $60 billion by 2025 and one-third of all congregations will fall victim to fraud. The number one deterrent of fraud is the fear of getting caught. As Lotich points out, it is just counterintuitive for a church to have the mindset that someone will steal from them. It goes beyond the inherent nature of love and trust.[4]

So, how are you feeling about the financial controls and management of your congregation? What are the chances that this is happening right now in your church? Do you have financial policies and procedures in place with adequate checks and balances? What are you willing to do to ensure that it does not happen in the future?

Take this brief assessment, and let's see if you are comfortable with your role as financial manager of your church.

CHURCH FINANCIAL MANAGEMENT ASSESSMENT

Church-related Financial Management

1. Do you have a comprehensive written policy that outlines all aspects of your ministry's financial procedures and controls?
2. Are the Statements of Financial Activity and Financial Position produced monthly?
3. Are these two statements reviewed thoroughly each month?
4. Do you have readily available financial reports for each ministry/department or project?
5. Do you operate with a budget and monitor variances regularly?
6. Are dual signatures required for withdrawals?
7. Have you separated the responsibilities of paying bills and reconciling the bank statement (minimum of two persons)?
8. Do you have more than one person counting the Sunday offering? And do you rotate this job?

9. Is the church reporting donations annually with the required IRS wording on the receipts?
10. Does your fiscal year-end accommodate your church schedule?

Pastor-related Financial Management

1. Is your payroll check handled according to the unique federal tax laws for ministers?
2. Are you paying self-employment taxes for FICA and Medicare?
3. Are you familiar with the federal tax laws related to your housing allowance?
4. Did you know you have a choice as to whether or not the church withholds your federal income tax?
5. Do you know if your church-related expenses are tax deductible?

While there are many more questions that might be asked, how did you do on the above? If you answered "No" or "I don't know" to any of these questions, please do not be embarrassed because it is not your area of expertise and in fact, it is unlikely any pastor would respond affirmatively to all the questions above.

Thomranier.com reported that the primary concerns of many pastors include more training regarding both business and personal finances. That is why I am passionate about sharing the knowledge I have and pointing you toward additional sources and/or experts in these areas.

Notes

1. http://hirr.hartsem.edu/research/fastfacts/fast_facts.html (accessed 9/2/17)
2. https://www.brotherhoodmutual.com/resources/safety-library/risk-management-articles/administrative-staff-and-finance/finances/church-fraud-embezzlement/ (accessed 8/11/17)
3. Ibid
4. https://sharefaith.com/blog/2015/09/18-church-embezzlement/ (accessed 8/11/17)

2

Lack of Knowledge

Be shepherds of God's flock that is under your care, watching over them—not because you must, but because you are willing, as God wants you to be; not pursuing dishonest gain, but eager to serve;
I Peter 5:2

To lead the church effectively, a pastor needs a basic knowledge of business, including a foundational understanding of financial terms, best practices, and important documents. Those who give want to know that the organization's leadership has a handle on the finances before they are willing to invest. One Christian university strongly encourages their theology students to minor in business, listing the number reason as "avoiding a mistake in finances." They point out this reality: no matter how strong the call of God is on your life or how hard you work, a mishandling of church funds can destroy your ministry.[1]

Googling the phrase "church embezzlement" brings up over 574,000 articles in the search results. And it appears that the thieves are no respecter of denomination or church size. Brotherhood Mutual Insurance has insured churches and related ministries for over 100 years and they report, "It doesn't take a hardened criminal to steal money from a church."[2]

In fact, those who embezzle are often *well-known, well-liked, and completely trusted by fellow church members*. They don't set out to steal hundreds, or even thousands, of dollars. But ample opportunity and lack of financial controls enable them to do just that. Unfortunately, many churches do not have sufficient internal controls and leave their financial manager unsupervised in an unregulated environment. As the pastor, it is ultimately your responsibility to protect yourself, your congregation, and the treasurer from the temptation that may arise from financial carelessness.

Most smaller churches depend on willing members, who likely already have a full schedule, to take on various church functions. If you are lucky their church 'job' will only be their second priority and not their third, fourth or even further down on their list. They handle Sunday collections, offering counts, deposits, and recordkeeping. These volunteers are necessary and depending on volunteers is not in and of itself a bad thing. However, many times these persons have no bookkeeping experience, are not properly trained, and are unaware of or even naïve about financial controls. Furthermore, since they are part of the church family, they are inherently trusted. This frame of mind places churches in the most vulnerable state for theft, embezzlement, and fraud.

The cliché "The church is not a museum of saints but a hospital for sinners," is especially poignant to this discussion. Temptation doesn't stay outside the church walls; it accompanies each member right through the front door. Add to that, the state of most American's personal finances. It has been estimated that over 25 percent have no monies set aside for emergencies, and almost half would not be able to cover an unexpected expense of $500.[3] Thus, that basket full of cash becomes the perfect carrot for the enemy to dangle. And the flesh is weak. As shepherd of the flock, it is your responsibility to ensure that controls are in place to make it difficult — if not impossible — for someone to succumb to this temptation.

American sociologist Donald R. Cressey describes the framework that allows a trusted individual to commit fraud in his theory "The Fraud Triangle."[4] His model explains most abuse that we refer to as fraud or embezzlement. The three components he discusses are Pressure, Opportunity, and Rationalization.

> 1-Pressure describes an external hardship that gives the "trust violator" (Cressey's term) motive. The person perceives this situation (usually financial) as one he or she cannot share with the organization. This financial trouble may be due to:
>
> • Sudden financial crisis, i.e. medical, housing, loss of employment
> • Devastating level of debt
> • Personal addiction to gambling, shopping, drugs, etc.
> • Feeling overworked and underpaid, or
> • Simply greed.
>
> 2-Opportunity occurs because this individual has reached a certain level of trust within the organization and is therefore not properly audited or supervised. Or perhaps, the organization

has no written policies and procedures in place with appropriate internal controls.

3- Rationalization seals the deal for the embezzler as this is the point in time when he or she can justify the crime by processing it through the filter of a defective moral compass and the perceived pressure(s) described above. Trust violators may even perceive themselves as victims of their circumstances rather than as thieves.

Once embezzlement begins, it is like the proverbial slippery slope without brakes, picking up speed on the way down. Whether fraudsters take a few dollars by mistake or out of desperation and no one notices, it becomes easier and easier to do it again and again until they find themselves in over their heads with no way to reverse their actions. As I am writing this today, I received a telephone call from a friend telling me that $5,000 has gone missing from their church and church leadership doesn't know what happened.

So, how does this specifically happen? Let's explore this in the next chapter.

FRAUD BY THE NUMBERS

David Barrett, an Episcopal missionary, pioneered religious demographics including finances. Several years ago, Barrett began including a line item in his global church balance sheet for "ecclesiastical crimes." He worked closely with Dr. Todd Johnson of the Center for the Study of Global Christianity who observed that "probably 80% of all cases are kept private or swept under the carpet."[5]

> The January 2017 issue of The International Bulletin of Mission Research reports that religious financial fraud is growing, estimating ecclesiastical crime will reach $59 billion in 2017. That calculates to almost $162 million per day. And they report that it is plausible to extrapolate the recent Association of Certified Fraud Examiners (ACFE) figures to Christian giving; thus, conservatively estimating that by the year 2025 global embezzlement of giving by Christians might be as high as $100 billion per year.[6]

Notes

1. https://www.sagu.edu/thoughthub/8-reasons-ministry-students-should-minor-in-business (accessed 8/14/17)
2. https://www.brotherhoodmutual.com/resources/safety-library/risk-management-articles/administrative-staff-and-finance/finances/church-fraud-embezzlement/ (accessed 8/11/17)
3. https://www.creditdonkey.com/average-american-savings-statistics.html (accessed 8/27/17)
4. https://www.hrzone.com/hr-glossary/what-is-the-fraud-triangle (accessed 1/11/18) Note: This theory does not apply to a person who enters an organization with the sole purpose to steal.
5. http://christiansentinel.com/2017/07/01/balance-sheet-global-christianity/ (accessed 8/15/17)
6. http://www.gordonconwell.edu/ockenga/research/Quick-Facts-about-Global-Christianity.cfm#embezzle (accessed 8/15/17)

3

Lack of Controls: Embezzlement, Fraud, and Theft

Jesus told them another parable: "The kingdom of heaven is like a man who sowed good seed in his field. But while everyone was sleeping, his enemy came and sowed weeds among the wheat, and went away. When the wheat sprouted and formed heads, then the weeds also appeared."
Matthew 13:24-26

Certified Church and Clergy Tax instructor Dr. Ronnie Shaw said, "You get what you inspect – not what you expect."[1] Instituting the proper controls and having independent verification offer the most likely means of avoiding embezzlement, fraud, or theft. And sadly, today's churches are plagued by all of these.

The Association of Certified Fraud Examiners (ACFE) published "The Fraud Tree" infographic that breaks out fraud into these categories:[2]

- Corruption: a scheme in which a volunteer/employee misuses their influence in a business transaction that violates their duty to gain direct or indirect benefit
- Asset Misappropriation: a scheme by which a volunteer/employee steals or misuses the organization's resources (cash or other assets)
- Financial Statement Fraud: "cooking the books" to hide expenditures, understate revenue, etc.

Let's dig deeper into what the ACFE points out about each of these three areas.

CORRUPTION

Corruption accounts for more than 35 percent of fraud cases investigated. This category covers conflict of interest schemes, bribery, illegal gratuities, and even economic extortion. Reviewing actual cases, it seems that conflict of interest and bribery are the most common types of corruption in the church.[3]

Conflict of interest involves exploiting authority to benefit self or someone else; for example, directing church business to a brother-in-law's printing company for the benefit of their family. Caution is needed here because such business transactions do not automatically mean that corruption is involved. Perhaps his company offers the best price, or they are the only vendor.

The safeguard here is to ensure that your procurement process is documented, with a special review when there is a familial connection; and therefore, the relationship is documented and the business transaction is properly vetted.

Another form of conflict of interest entails hiring a family member, friend, or friend's family member for a position in the church when they are not the most qualified candidate. Is there documentation that this person is the best choice for the position? Were other persons considered for the position? A well-written job description, application intake guidelines, and interview process will ensure that there is no appearance of impropriety, regardless of who the chosen employee is related to.

Bribery also falls under the category of corruption. Our inherent value of trust in the church makes any of these schemes seem impossible, but invoice kickbacks and even bid-rigging are not unheard of in church business. The organization must have policies and procedures in place to diminish the chances of this ever happening. One such policy might be to require that three bids are obtained before making a purchasing decision, as well as requiring a re-bid on an annual basis.

ASSET MISAPPROPRIATION

More than 83 percent of all fraud involves some type of asset misappropriation — a scheme by which a volunteer, a member, or an employee steals or misuses the organization's resources. 'Resources' refers to cash or other funds and all other assets such as tangible property. ACFE breaks this category down further:[4]

- Theft of Cash Receipts via
  - Skimming
  - Larceny
- Fraudulent Disbursements via
  - Billing Schemes

- Payroll Schemes
- Expense Reimbursement Schemes
- Check Tampering
- Register Disbursements (think Money Box)
- Credit/Debit Card Cyber Theft

• Physical/Tangible good Misappropriation via

- Misuse
- Larceny

When we break out and break down all the various methods for fraud, theft, and physical misappropriation of assets, the answer to the common question, *"How can this happen?"* becomes more clear.

Let's first define skimming versus larceny. Skimming means stealing the money before it is recorded in the accounts. Larceny involves stealing the money after it has been counted and recorded in the church's records.

Skimming in a church environment might be as simple as an usher taking cash out of the plate as they walk down the stairs from the balcony. It could be the person counting your offering each week borrowing some of the cash for their household emergency with full intentions of putting it back in the next week.

I spoke to a woman just this week who is on the church "counting team." She and one other person count the offering every Monday morning. The other team member has been doing this for 20 years. They then turn the count over to one individual who records the deposit. Any of those three persons could pocket some of the cash before it is recorded.

Another common occurrence vulnerable to skimming is direct receipt of money by an individual in church leadership. This might happen before, during, or after an activity simply out of convenience. Both the giver and receiver have good intentions of the money being used for a church program, but how do you ensure this donation makes it to the church's funds?

Larceny occurs when a church credit card is used for personal reasons. Consider the following questions. Do you require all church credit/debit card charges be supported with receipts each and every month? What rules and oversight do you have in place to ensure each of these card transactions is authorized and legitimate?

These are "easy" ways to commit larceny. Someone with imagination and little or no oversight can go way beyond these methods. For example, forged invoices for "church" expenditures or even real invoices of personal expenditures could be submitted for reimbursement. I have even heard of a church member purchasing gift cards at a local store and then using those for personal purchases. The credit card statement showed the store name and the church assumed the purchases were for the church.

Tangible properties of the church are stolen or misused as well. Does your church have a policy regarding borrowing church furnishings and equipment? If not, you run the risk of discovering a piece of equipment is not functioning or even missing the next time you need it. And if your church's legal entity is a 501(c)(3), you risk losing that status if you allow the use of the organization's assets for personal reasons.

FINANCIAL STATEMENT FRAUD

Financial statement fraud involves overstating the church's income or worth or understating the church's expenses or liabilities. Either type of fraudulent bookkeeping makes the church's financial position appear stronger than it actually is.

Overstating the church's income or worth is simply fabricating income. This is almost impossible to accomplish if you have an independent party reconciling your bank deposits to donation records. This hinges on having a system in place to record donation reports and segregating the donation recordkeeping from the reconciling.

Understating the church's expenses or liabilities may be as simple as not recording or paying payroll taxes. Or perhaps the financial secretary is not recording or paying the credit card balance each month. It would also be possible to completely omit a liability from the balance sheet. Unfortunately, this is a fairly easy fraud: open a credit card in the church's name, make charges, and record payments under various ministries. As long as the thief was not too greedy, they could maintain this practice for years.

Furthermore, when the person(s) maintaining your records has too little oversight, too much access, and the accounting system is not double-entry, it becomes easy to steal and cover it up with creative accounting. Anyone (think church treasurer, financial secretary, or administrative assistant) can change a cell on a spreadsheet to be anything they want it to be.

John warns us, "The thief comes only to steal and kill and destroy..." (John 10:10a). The temptations created by our lax church policies are often too strong for a mere human when they are in a desperate situation or just engulfed with a spirit of greed. By not having strong internal financial controls, active oversight, and even independent verification, pastors expose themselves, their volunteers, and their congregation to potential heartache and even destruction. Weeds can overtake the good grass if left unchecked and uninhibited.

So, how do you protect or defend the church's assets? The next chapter will discuss this important subject.

FRAUD IN THE NEWS

A former employee of the Wisconsin Conference of the United Methodist Church was sentenced to two years in prison for embezzling more than $158,000 from the organization. [5]

A New Hampshire man was sentenced to 46 months for embezzling more than $1.6 million from the Portsmouth Church of Christ Scientist. [6]

A volunteer church treasurer and his wife had been members of a Syracuse, New York congregation for over 12 years when it was discovered they had embezzled more than $505,000 by writing checks to the church's bank and then using those checks to purchase certified bank checks for personal use. He had never presented any documentation to the church board other than spreadsheets. He was sentenced to 15 years in state prison and ordered to pay restitution. His excuse was they had "financial issues." [7]

The woman who had served over two years as treasurer in St. Joseph, Michigan was ordered to pay $42,055 in restitution for embezzling from her church. Some checks from church members were cashed but no records kept that they were received. She was writing unauthorized checks to herself from the church's account to pay her bills.[8]

A Wisconsin church treasurer pleaded guilty one count of felony theft, admitting responsibility for over $190,000 use of unauthorized funds from her church. She used funds donated for mission trips.[9]

Notes

1. https://cmtc.org/is-embezzlement-happening-in-your-church/ (accessed 8/15/17)
2. http://www.acfe.com/rttn (accessed 8/21/17)
3. Ibid.
4. Ibid.
5. Miller, M. (March 4, 2004). "2-Year Sentence for Church Fraud; Former Employee Embezzled $158,000." Madison Capital Times. p. 4B
6. Staff. (July 22, 2003). "Man sentenced in church embezzlement." Boston Globe. p. B2
7. www.fraud-magazine.com/article.aspx?id=4294994725
8. http://www.freep.com/story/news/local/michigan/2017/07/12/michigan-church-funds-theft/471133001/
9. http://www.hudsonstarobserver.com/news/crime-and-courts/4275441-former-church-treasurer-enters-guilty-plea-embezzlement-case

PART II

Practical Solutions

4

Internal Controls

Put on the full armor of God, so that you can take your stand against the devil's schemes. For our struggle is not against flesh and blood, but against the rulers, against the authorities, against the powers of this dark world and against the spiritual forces of evil in the heavenly realms. Therefore, put on the full armor of God, so that when the day of evil comes, you may be able to stand your ground, and after you have done everything, to stand.
Ephesians 6:11-13

The old saying "the best defense is a good offense" is no less true for financial controls than it is for sports. Safeguarding your congregation's assets begins with effective, documented, and audited policies and procedures to reduce the opportunities for fraud.

A system of checks and balances known as internal controls can prevent an embezzler from stepping on that slippery slope and keep temptation at a safe distance. For instance, if the person taking care of the bank reconciliation does not also have access to the church funds or credit card, the opportunities for him or her to misuse funds and cover tracks are reduced. Internal controls are not completely foolproof, but they will significantly decrease the risk of embezzlement or fraud.

Examples of these types of controls are:

Physical:

- Locking up blank checks
- Protecting IDs and passwords (i.e. do not write them down!)
- Turning off computers at night so IDs and passwords have to be re-entered each day
- Using offering boxes (locked and secured to wall) vs. passing plates

Procedural:

- Requiring dual signatures on checks over a nominal amount
- Forbidding pre-signed checks and rubber stamp signatures
- Forming "counting teams" to serve on a random, rotating basis for Sunday offerings
- Segregating the money handling responsibility from the bank reconciliation function
- Performing background and credit checks on the leadership team and any person handling funds
- Reviewing all expenditures monthly for appropriate receipts and supporting documentation

- Establishing term limits for financial committee members and leadership team
- Requiring mandatory vacation for the regular bookkeeper
- Ensuring third parties with access to the office (maintenance, cleaners, etc.) are bonded and insured

Budgeting and Reporting:

- Budgeting expenditures by ministry
- Forecasting monthly receipts using historical data
- Reviewing the financial reports thoroughly each month looking for
  - Decrease in donations
  - Increase in expenses
  - Variance from budget

PROTECT YOURSELF

Too often the pastor is put in the position of managing the church finances. Even if he desires this responsibility, a pastor should never handle the money. He should take care to avoid even receiving a check by a member of the congregation. Pastors must remain "above reproach," which means it's best that they not even have signatory authority on the checking account.

On the other hand, the pastor should be financially astute enough to participate proactively in the budgeting process as well as understanding the financial statements. Some of the initial squabbles in the first-century church had to do with how the money was to be handled. (Acts 6:2-4) Wise management of the church's wealth is essential to the church's health. In the role of chief administrator of the church, it is important that the pastor has the appropriate knowledge to ask the right questions of those he puts in charge of the details.

It would be good practice for the pastor to have a monthly meeting with the financial statement preparer every month — whether in-person, online video, or via telephone. Be prepared to ask questions and request more detail. Consider making it a standard practice to have your financial preparer report on predetermined positive or negative percentage variances in actual amounts as compared to budgeted figures. Ask him or her to give you the detailed transaction list for random accounts each month.

PROTECT YOUR CONGREGATION

Donors want assurance that their gifts are supporting the purposes they intended. No one wants to finance an organization that is not properly caring for those funds

The annual church business meeting is probably not anyone's favorite hour of the year, but it certainly is an important one. Information is key to building trust, solving problems, setting goals, formulating opinions, evaluating sources, and making decisions. And it is possible to make financial information an integral and interesting part of your church's on-going agenda.

Transparency, a term used rather often these days, is truly a deterrent to fraud as well. Educating your congregation about finances will mean more financial watchdogs. And often it is a "tip" that will lead to the uncovering of fraud.

Being transparent with the church's finances accomplishes so many things:

- Giving a congregation confidence in the leadership's accountability
- Making it more difficult for fraud to occur
- Demonstrating the cyclical nature of giving
- Encouraging more giving
- Discouraging poor money management
- Providing prayer points for the congregation
- Making persons aware of ministries that need support

As you nominate new leadership team members at your annual meeting, you should consider:

- Selecting at least one person with a financial management background to serve on the leadership team.
- Holding a board boot camp session to orientate the leadership team on the church's policies and procedures as well as financial records, budgets, and statement reviews.
- Including credit and background checks as standard procedure on a regular and repeated basis.
- Establishing term limits for the leadership team and the financial committee.

And finally, procure a fidelity bond for your congregation. This is an inexpensive form of insurance protection that covers policyholders for losses they incur as a result of fraudulent acts by specified individuals.

PROTECT THE TREASURER (OR OTHER VOLUNTEER)

The church treasurer, financial secretary, or administrative assistant taking care of finances has a significant amount of responsibility. A lack of documented financial policies and procedures often exacerbates the situation and creates a burdensome position that not many can handle. In addition, too often this one individual is expected to handle all the financial matters which creates a situation ripe for fraud. Verify this person has experience. Vet the references and prior work history. Perform both criminal and credit checks on any person handling monies or financial records.

The traditional accounting/bookkeeping process has been revolutionized in the last few years, but many churches have yet to jump on this new high-speed train. They continue to run on the old locomotive, shoveling coal into the engine as fast as they can but not getting any more power. One copy of a software program on one computer is susceptible to data corruption, obsolescence, and manipulation as there is only one set of eyes on the data.

Implementing these new tools or "technology stacks," a combination of software and online applications, automates many functions that used to be done manually. The accounting process is changing and making life simpler for clients. This technology is so efficient and priced so reasonably now that if you consider the opportunity cost and fraud risk of having a treasurer do many of these tasks, it is really a no-brainer to look into jumping on this new train.

There are literally dozens of software applications that will make the responsibility of maintaining your financial records simpler and safer.

Some bookkeeping firms now specialize in determining the optimal "stack" for your needs and these nominally priced subscriptions are never outdated so you don't have to be concerned about large expenditures for software every couple of years. Another great advantage is that rather than one software program on one desktop, you have online and mobile accessibility for your entire church leadership team 24/7/365.

Here are a few of my favorite applications that work together to practically automate your accounting:

- *QuickBooks Online*: Double-entry accounting software with reports accessible by church leadership at home, at work, or on their mobile device. And yes, you can do fund accounting in QuickBooks.

- *Hubdoc*: Fetches all banking and credit card statements automatically, allows congregants or ministry leaders to submit receipts on their smartphones, and serves as a secure and permanent file cabinet that can be accessed and audited by your financial committee.

- *Bill.Com*: Allows you to automatically receive and route vendor bills for approval to church leadership and ultimately process payments.

You may already be using QuickBooks Online and perhaps even offering an online giving option via your website. But are you syncing these two technologies to drive greater efficiency and accuracy in your giving records? This will free-up staff, free-up volunteers, improve accountability and lessen the risk of fraud.

What else can you do to improve your financial operations? Let's look at chapter 5 on budgeting.

5

Budget Planning and Review

Jesus told his disciples: "There was a rich man whose manager was accused of wasting his possessions. So he called him in and asked him, 'What is this I hear about you? Give an account of your management, because you cannot be manager any longer.'"
Luke 16:1-2

Norman Vincent Peale said, "Plan your work and work your plan. Lack of system produces that 'I'm swamped' feeling." Avoiding that sense of being overwhelmed is only one of the reasons that budgeting is so important for a congregation.

The financial management necessary to run a church is like running a business and this requires a carefully laid out plan for both operations systems and the financial policies and procedures that support them. Organizational budgets guide spending and propel goals to the finish line. They keep everyone on track.

Budget creation involves a detailed analysis of expectations and results. By creating an annual budget, a church intentionally examines the needs and goals of each department and ministry for the coming year. These are positioned next to a review of current performance. This is the time to analyze successes and less-than-stellar programs from the last year, as well as identify resource allocation for the coming year.

This process — carried out with great care once each year — will save hours of discussion about resource usage throughout the next twelve months. An approved budget gives the pastor and those delegated as ministry leaders the authority to exercise a certain amount of discretionary spending without further approval if they are operating within budget guidelines.

As a matter of fact, this budget should encourage ministry leaders to avoid unessential spending. Think of the budget as the bumpers at the bowling alley. Ministry leaders have an idea of the guidelines for their spending because they have a budget. This empowers them to lead their area while simultaneously establishing spending controls.

Stewardship is fostered when a church operates with a budget. Wisely using resources facilitates funding the congregation's current commitments and future projects as well as setting aside funds for replacements and maintenance. It sets the stage for informed decisions as the months pass.

A monthly review of the Statement of Financial Activity as compared to the approved budget is a good place to start. When differences between actual and budgeted amounts are significant (either high or low) for a given month — or vary greatly from a previous month — there is reason to question the financial records. Not all budget variances indicate a negative situation. As the year progresses, the leadership team may see the need to adjust the budget as circumstances and expectations change.

Does your church have all the relevant information you need to prepare the best budget possible? One factor to consider is this: are you tracking expenses by programs/ministries? This type of accounting is one of the advantages of the new tools mentioned in the previous chapter. Today's technology offers a simple and effective way to document the financial plan for each ministry in your church and ensure that it is accounted for properly.

Budgeting and careful, regular review of the budget will create accountability by ministry leaders to the leadership team and the leadership team to the congregation. Please take advantage of a suggested chart of accounts and budgeting example at our website: BellwetherChurchSolutions.com/Resources.

6

Formal Financial Processes and Reports

Know well the condition of your flocks, And pay attention to your herds.
Proverbs 27:23

A strong bookkeeping system, formal reporting process, and regular review schedule are essential to establishing accountability, fostering transparency, and deterring embezzlement. A full accounting plan ensures the pastor and other leadership are both accurately informed about the condition of "the flock" and are regularly considering the state of the church. It is marked by standards and activities such as:

- Double-entry bookkeeping
- Separating the receiving, the recording, and the spending of church funds
- Reconciling all bank, credit, loan, and payroll accounts each month

- Providing a full set of financial statements, and
- Reviewing those financial statements

STRONG BOOKKEEPING SYSTEM

A healthy plan will be built on industry best practices and have the following:

1. Accurate records

This begins with confirming that financial records accurately list all assets and liabilities. It includes accounting for the depreciation of the assets and the interest on the debt. The financial information must be correct and complete to facilitate best decisions.

2. Timely records

All income and expenditures must be recorded in the month they occur. Otherwise, it could be months down the road before it is discovered that a restricted account has been overspent, payroll taxes weren't sent in, or donations are far above or below budgeted amounts. Accounts should be reconciled each month as soon as statements are available from the bank, credit card, or online donation processor. Consistent monthly reporting will drive these timely processes.

3. Complete system

A methodical system is the foundation for accurate and timely records. Do you have a checklist for closing out the books each month? Is anyone reviewing the checklist? Pre-defined steps help ensure best practices such as:

- All checking account transactions are entered for the month.
- All credit card charges are accounted for in the appropriate ministries.
- Offerings are reported in the proper month (even those collected on the last day of the month).

Furthermore, a complete system provides for the recording of relevant financial records that may not be part of the day-to-day accounting. Under normal circumstances, there is a paper trail that reminds the bookkeeper to make an accounting entry, i.e. a receipt, a deposit slip, or a check. However, there are times when there is no paperwork.

Here are examples of entries that may be overlooked without a methodical system of checklists:

- Recording the accruing interest on the building loan
- Depreciating the furnishings on the proper schedule
- Expensing the monthly portion of prepaid yearly insurance
- Making quarterly payroll tax payments

FORMAL REPORTING PROCESS

In order to see the complete financial picture, churches need a formal reporting system with an established Chart of Accounts. Leadership and decision-makers should receive a Statement of Financial Position

(Balance Sheet), a Statement of Financial Activity (Income Statement), and a Budget Report. If applicable, they should also view a Restricted Funds Schedule.

The Statement of Financial Activity is normally of most interest to folks. This statement is a summary of all the monies coming into the organization (donations) and going out of the organization (expenses) during a given period of time. Budgeting for these activities was covered in chapter 5.

The Statement of Financial Position is a snapshot at a given point in time of the organization's overall financial status. It answers questions such as:

- What is the value of our assets?
- How much debt do we have?
- Are we setting aside monies for future needs?

REGULAR REVIEW SCHEDULE

The value of the system and reporting is diminished if no one is regularly and thoroughly reviewing the reports. It is important for the preparer to review his or her own processes and double check the numbers, but there must be additional reviewers. Furthermore, the pastor and leadership must be knowledgeable enough to understand the interactions between accounts. A meeting each month with the bookkeeper should be scheduled to go through the statements and identify any situations that need attention.

One final word of caution:

If there is only one person handling all of the monies then it is easy for that preparer to doctor the reports to cover up deception. As stated previously, the safeguard to this potential situation is a separation of duties. Furthermore, the interjection of an independent professional — who can both handle the financial functions and/or assist in reviewing the financials — is an excellent deterrent to fraud.

FINAL CONSIDERATIONS:

Even with the advent of new accounting options, many churches still use an old-fashioned ledger or digital spreadsheet. Summary documents don't give leadership the whole story. Without the appropriate system and information flow, ministry leaders cannot make informed and wise decisions.

Many smaller churches assume they cannot afford these latest tools. In the past, church accounting software was out of reach for smaller congregations, but the price has come down significantly. Partnering with professionals who use these new tools is now both easy and affordable.

Churches and pastors have choices. The next chapter discusses the various options for improving the accounting system and safeguarding the church against fraud.

7

Considerations Going Forward

His master replied, "Well done, good and faithful servant! You have been faithful with a few things; I will put you in charge of many things. Come and share your master's happiness!"
Matthew 25:23

Each of us has God-given talents and strengths. It is my earnest desire to hear these words from the Lord one day: "well done, good and faithful servant." I think about this often and it inspires me to make the most of what God has given me.

I imagine you feel the same way. Thus, caring properly for the resources your congregation is blessed with is likely high on your list — as it should be. So, let's recap your choices for this critical responsibility.

PASTOR

In the very first chapter, you read a description of all the many jobs a pastor holds as shepherd of the church. All too often this means he takes care of the church financial business as well. *I cannot emphasize strongly enough that this is not acceptable.* And perhaps not for the reasons you might be thinking. I am concerned about protecting the pastor.

The New Testament teaches that leadership in the local church is to be plural (Acts 14:23; 20:17; Titus 1:5) Plural leadership is a safeguard for all concerned. Shouldering all the responsibilities of a flock is too much for one person. The New Testament church example of delegating duties is a picture for today as well (Acts 6:1-6).

Beyond the workload and biblical example of delegation, when a pastor takes on the financial tasks, the situation becomes ripe for accusation due to an appearance of the lack of accountability. Furthermore, your vocational calling is to shepherd the flock, to walk with God, to preach and to teach and provide spiritual leadership. This doesn't mean that you ignore the financial needs and responsibilities, but rather wisely guard your time and delegate functional responsibilities with discernment.

VOLUNTEERS

The option of using volunteers for church financial management was discussed in chapter 4. These particular points are worth emphasizing again here:

- Is the volunteer qualified?

- What is the true opportunity cost of delegating this person to the accounting function when you can outsource this work in today's world for as little as a few hundred dollars per month?
- What are the effects on you, the congregation, and the individual when fraud is discovered or simply rumored? Is it worth any amount of money to put someone in this position?
- And what about the legal nuances regarding church accounting – providing donation receipts in line with IRS guidelines and payroll tax reporting? Can you afford to put this in the hands of a volunteer?

PAID STAFF

This seems like a good alternative until you have to actually hire someone. What skills do they need? How much experience can you afford? Are they familiar with church finances? What if you hire the wrong person – then you have to actually fire someone? And in fact, a paid staff person presents the same concerns as listed above for volunteers.

And, perhaps even more importantly, there is the consideration of the current staff (paid and volunteers). Organizational culture is a system of shared assumptions, values, and beliefs. These shared values have a strong influence on the people in the organization and how they behave. Will this new person fit into your culture?

And, honestly, is one person enough? Has hiring this one person allowed you to effectively segregate the financial collection, recording and spending responsibilities enough to narrow significantly the opportunities for embezzlement and fraud? Not to mention, whose responsibility is it to keep this person busy? To supervise, encourage and train them? Some studies show the maximum productivity for a paid employee is less than three hours a day even though they are paid for eight.[1] Do you want to spend your time in administration or on your congregation?

And lastly, have you considered the true cost of hiring staff? It is not just the hourly or salaried wages you are paying them. You must add on any insurance coverage offered, workers compensation, payroll taxes (both Social Security and Medicare). What about the additional space, phone and office supplies they will need? It is normal to budget an additional 35 to 50 percent in addition to the actual salary of an individual as the true cost of hiring.

Until the last decade, these three options may have been the only choices. However, as we discussed in previous chapters new technology and tools have now made a fourth option both effective and affordable.

VIRTUAL OUTSOURCING

This option allows you to hire an expert without paying for more than you need by outsourcing your church's financial accounting to a specialty firm. You get expert eyes on your finances while you and your people are given the opportunity to focus on ministry. With modern technology, the cost of outsourcing is much less than you probably imagine.

Outsourcing the technical bookkeeping function offers your congregation consistent and committed financial assistance in contrast to the scenarios described above. A specialist in accounting for churches will provide you with the comfort and security of knowing dedicated, efficient, and accountable professionals are handling your church's financial matters correctly. And you are only paying for the hours worked!

An outsourcing accounting/bookkeeping provider has already spent the time and resources to bring you the best practices via policies and procedures as well as state-of-the-art bank-level security tools. They can help you put the "people" policies in place to maximize efficiency and function while adding that extra level of insurance to protect the church assets. They will help you determine what technology stack will work best for your organization. The collaborative processes made possible by this digital age are truly amazing.

Specialty firms like Bellwether Church Solutions can save you money, save you time, and more importantly save you from the heartache of fraud.

You have choices. Think about it. Research it. Pray about it. Simplify your life, protect your assets, empower your congregation, free up your staff and work for the Kingdom.

Notes

1. https://www.inc.com/melanie-curtin/in-an-8-hour-day-the-average-worker-is-productive-for-this-many-hours.html (accessed 10/10/17)

About the Author

Lee Ann Crockett is the founder of Bellwether Church Solutions. She believes everything she has done in her life has led her to this moment, this time, this vocation. She grew up in a family of pastors and church volunteers. After graduating from The University of Texas at Austin and attaining her CPA, she worked in auditing and management consulting for over 14 years in the corporate arena. She left her Fortune 100 career to raise her family but continued in small business consulting, non-profit volunteer and paid positions, and teaching. She retired her CPA, thinking grandparenting was her new career, when the Lord placed an irrepressible desire to come alongside churches with the tools that will alleviate administrative burdens and help them protect their assets.

Bellwether Church Solutions

bellwether | noun | bell•weth•er
1. one that takes the lead or initiative: leader;
also an indicator of trends
2. the leading sheep of a flock, with a bell on its neck.

Bellwether Church Solutions is a technology-driven bookkeeping provider that helps churches and non-profits meet their administrative needs and add layers of protection for their assets.

Our Core Values

- Put God first
- Integrity
- Excellence
- Stewardship

Our Company Culture encourages

- Collaboration: to accomplish win-win's
- Innovation: to work effectively and efficiently

- Communication: to understand and respond appropriately
- Education: to equip and teach
- Appreciation: to be humble and grateful
- Expectations: to meet and exceed

For a complimentary and confidential analysis of your church's financial status quo, please go to: www.BellwetherChurchSolutions.com/Resources

Made in the USA
Coppell, TX
21 July 2022